"SKUNK"

By Lee Jacobs

BLACKBIRCH®
PRESS

THOMSON
™
GALE

San Diego • Detroit • New York • San Francisco • Cleveland • New Haven, Conn. • Waterville, Maine • London • Munich

For Sarah

For more information, contact
The Gale Group, Inc.
27500 Drake Rd.
Farmington Hills, MI 48331-3535
Or you can visit our Internet site at http://www.gale.com

Photo Credits: Cover, pages 3, 6, 9, 12, 13, 15, 22 © Thomas Kitchin & Victoria Hurst; back cover, pages 4, 6, 16-17 © Corel Corporation; pages 5, 7, 8, 10, 11, 18-19, 20, 23 © CORBIS; pages 6, 9, 19, 21 © Art Today; page 8 © Dr. Lloyd Glenn Ingles, CalAcademy Special Collections, California Academy of Sciences

LIBRARY OF CONGRESS CATALOGING-IN-PUBLICATION DATA

Jacobs, Lee.
  Skunk / by Lee Jacobs.
    v. cm. — (Wild America)
  Contents: The skunk's environment—The skunk body—Social life—Hunters and raiders—
  The mating game—Skunks and humans.
    ISBN 1-56711-641-8 (hardback: alk. paper)
  1. Skunks—Juvenile literature. [1. Skunks.] I. Title.
  QL737.C25 J34 2003
  599.76'8—dc21   2002003380

Printed in China
10 9 8 7 6 5 4 3 2 1

Contents

The striped skunk is the most common kind of skunk in North America.

Skunks are mammals that belong to the family Mephitidae. The scientific family name comes from the word mephitis, which means "bad odor" in Latin. Skunks used to be classified as part of the family Mustelidae. That family includes weasels, wolverines, and badgers. But scientists decided skunks had many unique characteristics and created a new family for them.

The striped skunk is the most common skunk in North America. It lives in southern Canada, most areas of the United States, and northern Mexico. Other species of skunk are spotted skunks, hog-nosed skunks, and hooded skunks.

Above: Weasels (left), badgers (center), and wolverines (right) used to be considered in the same family as skunks. **Below:** Spotted skunks are less common in North America than striped skunks.

Skunks can live in many different environments. They are found in woodlands, grasslands, farming areas, and even cities and towns. Skunks usually stay close to water. They almost never stray more than about 2 miles (3 km) from a water source. Skunks often remain within a home range of about a half-mile (1 km) during the day. They may travel a few more miles when they hunt at night. Males tend to cover more area than females, especially when searching for a mate.

This page: Skunks live nearly everywhere in North America. They are found in grasslands, in cities and towns, and anywhere else that is near water.

Skunks often find natural dens in which to live. They may occupy caves, hollow logs, and crevices among piles of rocks or along rocky ledges. Skunks also find dens in human-made structures. They burrow under stone walls and porches, or find safe places to sleep in empty buildings. Skunks may also build burrows. These burrows are usually about 3 feet (1 m) underground, with tunnels that connect to the surface. Instead of building their own den, skunks will often take over abandoned woodchuck burrows.

The inside of a skunk den is lined with dried grass and leaves to make a comfortable bed. Skunks normally stay in one home throughout the winter. In warm weather, they move from burrow to burrow.

Hollow logs, caves, and rock piles make good skunk dens.

The most noticeable feature of a striped skunk's body is its coloring. Covered in soft, dense black fur, these skunks have a thin white stripe between their eyes. A much wider white stripe usually begins on the forehead. This stripe runs down the back and, sometimes, down the tail. Striped skunks can have one

Left: A striped skunk can have one or two stripes on its back.
Below: A thin stripe on the forehead is a marking for a striped skunk

8

or two stripes. Skunks shed their fur each year between spring and fall.

A skunk's tail is bushy and long. It often has white fur mixed with black fur.

From its head to the beginning of its tail, an adult skunk measures about 12 to 18 inches (31 to 46 cm) long. The tail adds another 7 to 16 inches (18 to 40 cm) in length. The average skunk weighs between 5 and 15 pounds (2 to 7 kg). Males are usually a little larger than females.

Skunks walk flat-footed, with a slight waddle. A skunk's head is small. It has a pointy nose, sharp teeth, and little ears. Skunks have long, sharp claws on their front paws, which they use to dig for food.

Top: A skunk's tail is bushy and long.
Bottom: Long, sharp claws help skunks dig for food.

Special Features

Skunks are best known for the extremely bad smell they can have. A skunk has scent glands beneath its tail. These glands produce a sticky yellow substance called "musk." If another animal (including a human) scares or threatens a skunk, it will spray the musk to defend itself.

A skunk gives several warnings that it is about to spray. It will stamp its front feet to tell an enemy to back off. It may also raise its tail and hiss.

If these warnings don't scare the enemy away, the skunk then bends its body so that both its head and behind are facing the animal.

Skunks have powerful scent glands under their tails.

In this position, the skunk shoots two streams of musk (one from each gland) toward its target. A skunk can send its foul-smelling scent flying a distance of up to 12 feet (4 m)! And skunks have very good aim. They often direct the spray right into the eyes of their enemies.

The musk stings the target's nose and eyes and can blur its vision. It can also make the victim sick. It is also very hard to wash off.

If a skunk is being chased, it can spray a cloud of its scent. This usually stops the predator from continuing the hunt. Skunks will never spray their scent to attack an enemy. They only spray to defend themselves.

If it is in danger, a skunk will spray its foul-smelling musk into the eyes of an enemy.

11

Social Life

Adult skunks without young tend to keep to themselves much of the time. But family groups stick together. In the winter, a group of 5 or 6 female skunks may choose to den together. Sometimes a male skunk will be allowed to join them. Skunks do not hibernate (sleep through the winter). But they do spend a lot of time sleeping in their winter dens. They do not eat much between November and March. By spring, most skunks have lost some of their body weight.

Skunks do not hibernate in winter.

Skunks use a variety of different sounds to communicate with each other. When angry, upset, or afraid, they growl, hiss, or make a whirring kind of sound. An excited skunk may squeal. A contented skunk may make a cooing sound.

Male skunks sometimes use their spray to communicate. A male skunk may spray to mark its territory or to get a female's attention during mating season.

An excited skunk may squeal or hiss.

Hunters and Raiders

Skunks are mainly nocturnal animals, which means they sleep during the day and are active at night. Striped skunks spend most of the night hunting. They are omnivores, which means they eat both animals and plants. In fact, skunks will eat almost anything they can find. They will even eat carrion (dead or decaying animals). A skunk's good senses of smell and hearing help it to locate food.

Skunks eat a varied diet. They will eat mice, shrews, frogs, lizards, snakes, fruits, nuts, plant buds, birds, insects, and garbage. They use their sharp claws to dig up beetles, earthworms, snails, and grubs (larvae form of beetles). A skunk will even bat at a honeybee nest to disturb the occupants inside. Once the bees fly out, the skunk swipes them up and swallows them.

Skunks also like to eat the eggs of turtles, birds, and chickens. A skunk will raid a bird's nest and break open the shells to eat the eggs. Skunks can also swim. They are skilled at catching small fish from rivers and ponds.

Skunks like to eat bird eggs. They will often raid a nest that is not being guarded.

A skunk's spray helps it fend off many predators (animals that hunt other animals for food). But bobcats, foxes, great horned owls, eagles, dogs, and coyotes all eat skunks.

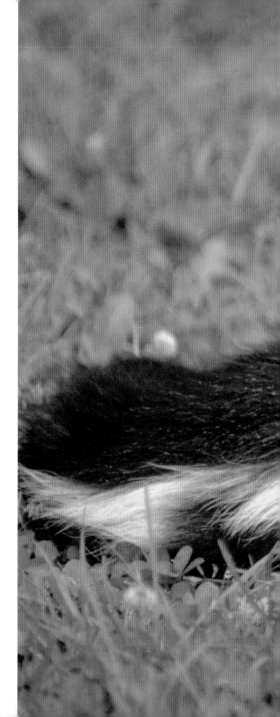

Male and female skunks do not spend much time together until it is time to breed. Mating season is from late winter to early spring. Females are able to reproduce within their first year of life. Younger mothers give birth to fewer babies than older mothers.

A male will travel for a long distance to find a mate and will breed with several females. Males often fight each other over mating partners. After mating, a female skunk will push the male out of her den. Males do not help raise skunk babies.

Males and females come together for mating in late winter and early spring.

A female skunk is pregnant for about 60 days. During this time, she often makes a den in a hollow tree where she can have her babies in safety. The babies are called "kits." Striped skunks may have 2 litters during a mating season. (A litter is one mother's group of baby animals all born at the same time.) Skunks have litters of between 2 and 10 babies.

Skunk babies are born with their black and white coloring, but it takes about 2 weeks for their hair to thicken into fur. They are born blind and deaf and are tiny. Each one weighs only about 1 ounce (28 g). When the kits are 3 weeks old, they weigh about 6 to 7 ounces (170 to 198 g). At this age, the kits open their eyes and start crawling. Mother skunks nurse their kits for 7 or 8 weeks. When the kits are about two months old, the mother will take them out of the den on their first hunting trip. The babies are able to spray their musk at this age if they need to.

Kits are born with their coloring, but are blind and deaf.
Inset: A skunk mother prepares a den before her babies are born.

19

Rock crevices, hollow logs, and woodchuck burrows are common birthing places.

When they are away from their den, kits often follow after their mothers in single file. Mother skunks teach their young how to defend themselves against predators. The kits will playfully fight with each other, practicing important skills for when they are older. A mother skunk is always on the lookout for danger. If she senses trouble, she will stamp her feet. This signals the kits to quickly return to the safety of their den.

Mothers also teach their young how to hunt and dig for food. Kits stay with their mother until they are about 6 months old. By fall, the babies are nearly adult in size. Most are ready to go off on their own. Sometimes a few kits, usually females, stay with their mothers for the winter.

Inset: Baby skunks stay close together and follow their mothers until they are 6 months old.

People often complain about the trouble skunks can cause. If threatened by a family pet, a skunk will spray. Skunk spray is very hard to get rid of—especially on a longhaired dog! Several baths in vinegar or tomato juice may be needed before the smell goes away. Skunks also dig up yards and gardens looking for juicy insects to eat. They may get into a farmer's chicken coop and eat both the eggs and the chickens. Skunks can also carry a deadly virus called rabies. They can pass this on through a bite. Family cats and dogs should be given shots to protect them against rabies.

Humans generally consider skunks to be pests.

Skunks are useful to humans because they eat rodents and insects that can ruin crops.

Even though people think of them as pests, skunks are also helpful to humans. They kill rodent pests such as rats and mice. Skunks also help farmers by eating large numbers of insects, such as grasshoppers, that would otherwise ruin crops.

The most important thing to remember about skunks is that they are wild animals. If they feel threatened or scared, they will spray and might even bite. They may look cute and cuddly, but these fascinating creatures should only be observed from a safe distance.

Glossary

carrion dead or decaying animals
hibernate to sleep through the winter
kit a baby skunk
litter one mother's group of baby animals
    born at the same time
nocturnal active at night and asleep during
    the day

omnivore animals that eat plants and other
    animals
predator an animal that hunts another
    for food
prey an animal that is being hunted for food

Further Reading

Books

Biel, Timothy Levi. *Skunks and Their Relatives.* Mankato, MN: Creative Education, 1996.

Souza, D.M. *Skunks Do More Than Stink.* Brookfield, CT: Millbrook Press, 2002.

Swanson, Diane. *Welcome to the World of Skunks.* Portland, OR: Graphic Arts Center
  Publishing, 1999.

Web sites

*Striped Skunk—**http://wildunc.org/af/stripedskunk.html***

Index